To:

_____

From:

_____

Date:

_____

PROMISES &
BLESSINGS
FOR A
Sister's
HEART

Pi Pocket
INSPIRATIONS

summerside
PRESS

© 2012 Summerside Press™
Minneapolis, MN 55337
www.summersidepress.com

Promises & Blessings for a Sister's Heart

A *Pocket Inspirations* Book

ISBN 978-1-60936-659-9

Scripture references are from the following sources: The Holy Bible, New
International Version®, NIV®. Copyright © 1973, 1978, 1984, 2011 by
Biblica, Inc.™ Used by permission of Zondervan. All rights reserved worldwide.
The New King James Version (NKJV). Copyright © 1982 by Thomas Nelson,
Inc. Used by permission. Used by permission. The New American Standard
Bible® (NASB), Copyright © 1960, 1962, 1963, 1968, 1971, 1972, 1973,
1975, 1977, 1995 by The Lockman Foundation. Used by permission. Used by
permission. The Holy Bible, New Living Translation (NLT), copyright 1996,
2004, 2007 by Tyndale House Foundation. Used by permission of Tyndale
House Publishers, Inc., Carol Stream, Illinois 60188. The New Century Ver-
sion® (NCV). Copyright © 1987, 1988, 1991 by Thomas Nelson, Inc. Used
by permission. The Contemporary English Version® (CEV). Copyright © 1995
American Bible Society. *The Message* (MSG). Copyright © 1993, 1994, 1995,
1996, 2000, 2001, 2002 by Eugene Peterson. Used by permission of NavPress,
Colorado Springs, CO. All rights reserved.

Excluding Scripture verses and divine pronouns, in some quotations references
to men and masculine pronouns have been replaced with genderneutral or
feminine references. Additionally, in some quotations we have carefully updated
verb forms and wording that may distract modern readers.

Stock or custom editions of Summerside Press titles may be purchased in bulk
for educational, business, ministry, fundraising, or sales promotional use. For
information, please e-mail specialmarkets@summersidepress.com.

Designed by Lisa & Jeff Franke
Interior design by Jeff Jansen | aestheticsoup.net

*Summerside Press™ is an inspirational publisher offering fresh,
irresistible books to uplift the heart and engage the mind.*

Printed in USA.

Contents

Introduction

Family relationships, clothes, secrets,
disagreements, dreams—sisters share
so much. The secrets you never told
your parents. The photos you wish you
could hide. The dreams of your children
growing up together. The bond between
sisters is something incredibly special.

Promises & Blessings for a Sister's Heart is a
celebration of that bond. These warm messages
of joy and promises from God's Word
offer blessing after blessing for sisters
of any age. Full of encouragement,
gratitude, and insight, this little book
will find a tender spot in your heart.

May the bonds of sisterhood
only grow stronger as you live
out your lives together.

You Are God's Created Beauty

Let there be many windows in your soul,

That all the glory of the universe may beautify it.

ELLA WHEELER WILCOX

Today a new sun rises for me;
everything lives, everything is animated,
everything seems to speak to me of my passion,
everything invites me to cherish it.

ANNE DE LENCLOS

Stretch out your hand and take
the world's wide gift of joy and beauty.

CORINNE ROOSEVELT ROBINSON

The beauty of a woman is not in a facial mole,
But true beauty in a woman
is reflected in her soul.
It is the caring that she lovingly gives,
the passion that she shows,
And the beauty of a woman with passing years—
only grows!

SAM LEVENSON

The LORD is the portion of my inheritance
and my cup; You support my lot.
The lines have fallen to me in pleasant places;
Indeed, my heritage is beautiful to me.

PSALM 16:5–6 NASB

Something deep in all of us yearns for God's
beauty, and we can find it no matter where we are.

SUE MONK KIDD

Go outside, to the fields, enjoy nature and the
sunshine, go out and try to recapture happiness in
yourself and in God. Think of all the beauty that's
still left in and around you and be happy!

ANNE FRANK

Isn't it a wonderful morning?
The world looks like something God had
just imagined for His own pleasure.

LUCY MAUD MONTGOMERY

*W*hen God is personally present...
we are transfigured..., our lives gradually
becoming brighter and more beautiful as
God enters our lives and we become like Him.

2 CORINTHIANS 3:17–18 MSG

*T*he beauty of the world about us is only
according to what we ourselves bring to it.

BERTHA LINDSAY

*You are God's created beauty and the focus
of His affection and delight.*

JANET WEAVER SMITH

*M*ay God give you eyes to see beauty
only the heart can understand.

Nothing can compare to the beauty and greatness
of the soul in which our King dwells in
His full majesty. No earthly fire can compare with
the light of its blazing love. No bastions
can compare with its ability to endure forever.

TERESA OF AVILA

In all ranks of life the human heart yearns for
the beautiful, and the beautiful things that God
makes are His gift to all alike.

HARRIET BEECHER STOWE

You should clothe yourselves...with the beauty
that comes from within, the unfading
beauty of a gentle and quiet spirit,
which is so precious to God.

1 PETER 3:4 NLT

A sister is one who knows you as you really are,
understands where you've been, accepts who
you've become, and still gently invites you
to grow into a beauty all your own.

As God's workmanship, we deserve
to be treated, and to treat ourselves,
with affection and affirmation,
regardless of our appearance or performance.

MARY ANN MAYO

The future belongs to those who believe
in the beauty of their dreams.

ELEANOR ROOSEVELT

Beauty puts a face on God. When we gaze at
nature, at a loved one, at a work of art,
our soul immediately recognizes
and is drawn to the face of God.

MARGARET BROWNLEY

The Joys We Share

How sweet the sound of sisters laughing together,
of sharing the joy of knowing each other so well.

The God of the universe—
the One who created everything
and holds it all in His hands—created each
of us in His image, to bear His likeness,
His imprint. It is only when Christ
dwells within our hearts, radiating the pure
light of His love through our humanity,
that we discover who we are and what
we were intended to be. There is no other joy
that reaches as deep or as wide or as high—
there is no other joy that is more complete.

Sisters are for sharing laughter
and wiping tears.

When sisters stand shoulder to shoulder,
who stands a chance against us?

PAM BROWN

But let all who take refuge in you be glad; let them ever sing for joy. Spread your protection over them, that those who love your name may rejoice in you.

PSALM 5:11 NIV

If one is joyful, it means that one is faithfully living for God, and that nothing else counts; and if one gives joy to others one is doing God's work. With joy without and joy within, all is well.

JANET ERSKINE STUART

Add to your joy by counting your blessings.

The gift of friendship—both given and
received—is joy, love and nurturing for the heart.
The realization that you have met a soul mate…
a kindred spirit…a sister…a true friend…
is one of life's sweetest gifts!

Our hearts were made for joy. Our hearts were
made to enjoy the One who created them.
Too deeply planted to be much affected by
the ups and downs of life, this joy is a knowing
and a being known by our Creator.
He sets our hearts alight with radiant joy.

You will show me the path of life;
in Your presence is fullness of joy;
At Your right hand are pleasures forevermore.

PSALM 16:11 NKJV

*H*ow necessary it is to cultivate a spirit of joy.
It is a psychological truth that the physical acts
of reverence and devotion make one feel devout.
The courteous gesture increases one's respect
for others. To act lovingly is to begin to feel loving,
and certainly to act joyfully brings joy to others
which in turn makes one feel joyful.
I believe we are called to the duty of delight.

DOROTHY DAY

*As we grow in our capacities to see and
enjoy the joys that God has placed in our
lives, life becomes a glorious experience
of discovering His endless wonders.*

If you don't understand how a woman
could both love her sister dearly
and want to wring her neck at the same time,
then you were probably an only child.

LINDA SUNSHINE

To be able to find joy in another's joy,
that is the secret of happiness.

The Lord has filled my heart with joy;
I feel very strong in the Lord....
I am glad because You have helped me!

1 SAMUEL 2:1 NCV

Reach out and care for someone who needs
the touch of hospitality. The time you spend
caring today will be a love gift that will blossom
into the fresh joy of God's Spirit in the future.

EMILIE BARNES

Blessings Overflow

Sisters are blossoms in the garden of life.

A close relationship with a sister is more than
camaraderie or companionship; it's a familiarity
of our self, a touching of souls.

I wished I had a box, the biggest I could find,
I'd fill it right up to the brim with
everything that's kind.
A box without a lock, of course, and never any key;
for everything inside that box would
then be offered free.
Grateful words for joys received I'd freely give away.
Oh, let us open wide a box of praise for every day.

*M*ay the LORD, the God of your ancestors,
increase you a thousand times
and bless you as he has promised!

DEUTERONOMY 1:11 NIV

*Let God's promises shine
on your problems.*

CORRIE TEN BOOM

How great is God's goodness
to have given me a sister like you!

Tarry at the promise till God meets you there.
He always returns by way of His promises.

L. B. COWMAN

Once someone held my hand
and wiped away a tear.
That someone very special was you,
my sister dear.

How abundant are the good things
that you have stored up for those
who fear you, that you bestow in the sight of all,
on those who take refuge in you.

PSALM 31:19 NIV

You go before me and follow me.
You place Your hand of blessing on my head.
Such knowledge is too wonderful for me,
too great for me to understand!

PSALM 139:5–6 NLT

*Within each of us, just waiting
to blossom, is the wonderful promise
of all we can be.*

A sister is one of the nicest things that can
happen to anyone.
She is someone to laugh with and share with,
to work with and join in the fun.
She is someone who helps in the rough times
and knows when you need a warm smile.
She is someone who will quietly listen
when you just want to talk for awhile.

*G*od has not promised sun without rain, joy
without sorrow, peace without pain.
But God has promised strength for the day, rest
for the labor, light for the way,
grace for the trials, help from above, unfailing
sympathy, undying love.

ANNIE JOHNSON FLINT

*L*ift up your eyes. Your heavenly Father
waits to bless you—in inconceivable
ways to make your life what you
never dreamed it could be.

ANNE ORTLUND

I thank God, my sister, for the blessing you are...
for the joy of your laughter...
the comfort of your prayers...
the warmth of your smile.

*S*ometimes I must drive her crazy.
But she loves me anyway and never lets on.
She continues to guard my heart and nurture
my soul. My sister is a true blessing in my life.

BETTY PEARL HOOPER

Someone to Laugh With

*It was nice growing up with someone
like you—someone to lean on,
someone to count on...someone to tell on.*

*T*ake time to laugh. It is the music of the soul.

*Blessed are they who can laugh
at themselves, for they shall never
cease to be amused.*

*H*e will yet fill your mouth with laughing,
and your lips with rejoicing.

JOB 8:21 NKJV

*S*ense of humor; God's great gift
causes spirits to uplift,
Helps to make our bodies mend;
lightens burdens; cheers a friend;
Tickles children; elders grin
at this warmth that glows within;
Surely in the great hereafter
heaven must be full of laughter!

If you can remain calm,
you just don't have all the facts.

A cheerful heart is good medicine.

PROVERBS 17:22 NIV

You can kid the world. But not your sister.

CHARLOTTE GRAY

Today's Forecast: Partly rational
with brief periods of coherent thought giving
way to complete apathy by tonight.

SHERRIE WEAVER

Whole-hearted, ready laughter heals,
encourages, relaxes anyone within hearing
distance. The laughter that springs from love
makes wide the space around—gives room
for the loved one to enter in.

EUGENIA PRICE

If I can be of any help,
you're in more trouble than I thought.

A good laugh is as good as a prayer sometimes.

LUCY MAUD MONTGOMERY

There's nothing wrong with having nothing
to say, as long as you don't say it out loud.

The best laughter, the laughter that can heal, the
laughter that has the truest ring, is the laughter
that flowers out of a love for life and its Giver.

MAXINE HANCOCK

In the world you will have tribulation;
but be of good cheer, I have overcome the world.

JOHN 16:33 NKJV

To err is human,
to blame your sister even more so.

People can be divided into three groups: Those
who make things happen, those who watch things
happen, and those who wonder what happened.

A sister is one who laughs at your jokes when
they're not very funny and sympathizes with your
problems when they're not very serious.

*If you can learn to laugh in spite of the
circumstances that surround you, you will
enrich others, enrich yourself, and more than
that, you will last!*

Barbara Johnson

I know my older sister loves me
because she gives me all her old clothes
and has to go out and buy new ones.

*L*aughing at ourselves as well as with each other
gives a surprising sense of togetherness.

HAZEL C. LEE

*W*e ought to be able to learn things secondhand.
There is not enough time for us to make all the
mistakes ourselves.

HARRIET HALL

*I*f your sister is in a tearing hurry
to go out and cannot catch your eye,
she's wearing your best sweater.

PAM BROWN

Ah...Contentment

The moments I love best
are the times I spend with you.

Contentment is not the fulfillment
of what you want, but the realization
of how much you already have.

Where the soul is full of peace and joy,
outward surroundings and circumstances
are of comparatively little account.

HANNAH WHITALL SMITH

We brought nothing into the world,
so we can take nothing out. But, if we have food
and clothes, we will be satisfied with that.

1 TIMOTHY 6:7–8 NCV

*When it's hard to look back,
and you're scared to look ahead, you can look
beside you and your sister will be there.*

Peace within makes beauty without.

ENGLISH PROVERB

Normal day, let me be aware of the treasure
you are. Let me learn from you, love you,
bless you before you depart. Let me not pass you
by in quest of some rare and perfect tomorrow.

The great advantage of living in a large family
is that early lesson of life's essential unfairness.

NANCY MITFORD

Life is not intended to be simply a round
of work, no matter how interesting
and important that work may be.
A moment's pause to watch the glory of a sunrise
or a sunset is soul satisfying, while a bird's song
will set the steps to music all day long.

LAURA INGALLS WILDER

Sometimes our hearts get tangled
And our souls a little off-kilter
Friends and family can set us right
And help guide us back to the light.

SERA CHRISTANN

Keep your lives free from the love of money
and be content with what you have,
because God has said, "Never will I leave you;
never will I forsake you."

HEBREWS 13:5 NIV

I am still determined to be cheerful and happy,
in whatever situation I may be; for I have also
learned from experience that the greater part
of our happiness or misery depends upon our
dispositions, and not upon our circumstances.

MARTHA WASHINGTON

The desire to be and have a sister is a primitive
and profound one that may have everything
or nothing to do with the family a woman
is born to. It is a desire to know and be known
by someone who shares blood and body,
history and dreams, common ground
and the unknown adventures of the future,
darkest secrets and the glassiest beads of truth.

ELIZABETH FISHEL

It is always wise to stop wishing for things
long enough to enjoy the fragrance
of those now flowering.

PATRICE GIFFORD

Godliness with contentment is great gain.

1 TIMOTHY 6:6 NKJV

Let the day suffice, with all its joys and failings,
its little triumphs and defeats. I'd happily,
if sleepily, welcome evening as a time of rest,
and let it slip away, losing nothing.

KATHLEEN NORRIS

Satisfy us in the morning with your unfailing love,
that we may sing for joy and be glad all our days.

PSALM 90:14 NIV

True contentment is a real, even an active, virtue—
not only affirmative but creative.
It is the power of getting out of any
situation all there is in it.

G. K. CHESTERTON

Love All Around

Heaven comes down to touch us when we find
ourselves safe in the heart of another.

There is no need to plead that the love of God
shall fill our hearts as though He were unwilling
to fill us.... Love is pressing around us
on all sides like air. Cease to resist it
and instantly love takes possession.

AMY CARMICHAEL

Love is reaching, touching and caring,
sharing sunshine and flowers,
so many happy hours together.

Love God, your God, walk in all His ways,
do what He's commanded, embrace Him,
serve Him with everything you are and have.

JOSHUA 22:5 MSG

No matter how far apart we are,
I'll always be thinking of you, my sister,
because you mean the world to me.

*What we have once enjoyed
we can never lose. All that we love deeply
becomes a part of us.*
HELEN KELLER

Loving a sister is an unconditional, narcissistic,
and complicated devotion that approximates
a mother's love...sisters are inescapably connected,
shaped by the same two parents,
the same trove of memory and experience.

MARY BRUNO

For You bless the Godly, O LORD;
You surround them with your shield of love.

PSALM 5:12 NLT

Open your hearts to the love God instills....
God loves you tenderly. What He gives you is not
to be kept under lock and key, but to be shared.

MOTHER TERESA

A sister is someone who knows all about you,
and still chooses not to go away.

*Love grows from our capacity to give
what is deepest within ourselves and also
receive what is the deepest within another
person. The heart becomes an ocean strong
and deep, launching all on its tide.*

Life's lasting joy comes in erasing the boundary
line between "mine" and "yours."

*L*ove makes burdens lighter, because you divide
them. It makes joys more intense, because you
share them. It makes you stronger, so that you
can reach out and become involved with life
in ways you dared not risk alone.

*O*nly He who created the wonders of the world
entwines hearts in an eternal way.

*L*ove...bears all things, believes all things,
hopes all things, endures all things.
Love never fails.

1 CORINTHIANS 13:4, 7–8 NKJV

*N*othing can separate you from His love,
absolutely nothing.... God is enough for time,
and God is enough for eternity. God is enough!

HANNAH WHITALL SMITH

Caring words, friendship, affectionate touch—
all of these have a healing quality.
Why? Becausewe were all created by God
to give and receive love.

JACK FROST

To love a person is to learn the song
that is in their heart, and to sing it to them
when they have forgotten.

Love in the heart wasn't put there to stay;
love isn't love 'til you give it away.

OSCAR HAMMERSTEIN II

The fountain of beauty is the heart,
and every generous thought illustrates
the walls of your chamber.

FRANCIS QUARLES

Encouragement Means Such a Lot

There are times when encouragement
means such a lot. And a word
is enough to convey it.

GRACE STRICKER DAWSON

A word of encouragement to those we meet, a cheerful smile in the supermarket, a card or letter to a friend, a readiness to witness when opportunity is given—all are practical ways in which we may let His light shine through us.

ELIZABETH B. JONES

*S*ome days, it is enough encouragement just to watch the clouds break up and disappear, leaving behind a blue patch of sky and bright sunshine that is so warm upon my face. It's a glimpse of divinity; a kiss from heaven.

When mom and dad don't understand, a sister always will.

*F*or there is no friend like a sister
    In calm or stormy weather;
To cheer one on the tedious way,
To fetch one if one goes astray,
To lift one if one totters down,
To strengthen whilst one stands.

CHRISTINA ROSSETTI

*B*y now we know and anticipate
one another so easily, so deeply,
    we unthinkingly finish
    each other's sentences,
    and often speak in code.
No one else knows what I mean
    so exquisitely, painfully well;
    no one else knows so exactly
    what to say, to fix me.

JOAN FRANK

*I'm sure now I'll see God's goodness
in the exuberant earth. Stay with God!
Take heart. Don't quit.*

PSALM 27:13 MSG

*More and more I realize that everybody,
regardless of age, needs to be hugged and
comforted in a brotherly or sisterly way now
and then. Preferably now.*

JANE HOWARD

*Calm me, O Lord, as You stilled the storm,
Still me, O Lord, keep me from harm.
Let all the tumult within me cease,
Enfold me, Lord, in Your peace.*

CELTIC TRADITIONAL

To help one another,
is part of the religion of sisterhood.

LOUISA MAY ALCOTT

Encouragement is being a good listener,
being positive, letting others know you accept
them for who they are. It is offering hope, caring
about the feelings of another, understanding.

GIGI GRAHAM TCHIVIDJIAN

Sisters lift our spirits and stick
with us when times are tough.

The comfort of knowing that our bond
will survive despite our differences and that our
connection provides each of us with a more
accurate picture of ourselves enhances
our chances of finding inner peace
and satisfaction as we age together.

JANE MERSKY LEDER

*N*ow may our Lord Jesus Christ Himself
and God our Father, who has loved us
and given us eternal comfort and good hope
by grace, comfort and strengthen your hearts
in every good work and word.

2 THESSALONIANS 2:16–17 NASB

*H*ope begins in the dark, the stubborn hope
that if you just show up and try to do
the right thing, the dawn will come. You wait
and watch and work: You don't give up.

ANNE LAMOTT

I wanted you to see what real courage is....
It's when you know you're licked
before you begin but you begin anyway
and you see it through no matter what.

HARPER LEE

Praise: A Perpetual Rejoicing

Happiness is a quiet,
perpetual rejoicing in small events.

*G*od specializes in things fresh and firsthand.
His plans for you this year may outshine
those of the past.... He's preparing to
fill your days with reasons to give Him praise.

JONI EARECKSON TADA

*L*et us give all that lies within us...
to pure praise, to pure loving adoration,
and to worship from a grateful heart—
a heart that is trained to look up.

AMY CARMICHAEL

*O*ur prayers should be burning words
coming forth from the furnace of a heart
filled with love. Devoutly, with great
sweetness, with natural simplicity,
without any affectation, offer your praise
to God with the whole of your heart and soul.

MOTHER TERESA

They that trust the Lord find many things
to praise Him for. Praise follows trust.

LILY MAY GOULD

May your life become one of glad
and unending praise to the Lord as you
journey through this world,
and in the world that is to come!

TERESA OF AVILA

Enter into His gates with thanksgiving,
And into His courts with praise.
Be thankful to Him and bless His name.

PSALM 100:4 NKJV

Sing the praises of the LORD,
you his faithful people; praise his holy name.

PSALM 30:4 NIV

If I were to make a solemn speech in praise of
you, in gratitude, in deep affection, you would
turn an alarming shade of crimson and try to
escape. So I won't. Take it all as said.

MARION C. GARRETTY

Let's praise His name! He is holy,
He is almighty. He is love. He brings hope,
forgiveness, heart cleansing, peace and power.
He is our deliverer and coming King.
Praise His wonderful name!

LUCILLE M. LAW

Thanksgiving puts power in living,
because it opens the generators of the heart
to respond gratefully, to receive joyfully,
and to react creatively.

The gift of praise is the best gift you can give your sister, any time of the year.

Heavenly Father, thank You for my wonderful family. Even though we are not perfect, I praise You for this group of people that You have ordained as those who will be closest to me.... Amen.

KIM BOYCE

We your people, the sheep of your pasture, will praise you forever; from generation to generation we will proclaim your praise.

PSALM 79:13 NIV

49

*M*orning has broken like the first morning,
Blackbird has spoken like the first bird....
Praise with elation, praise every morning,
God's re-creation of the new day!

ELEANOR FARJEON

*I*f we learn how to give of ourselves, to forgive
others, and to live with thanksgiving, we need not
seek happiness. It will seek us.

*O*ur thanksgiving today should include
those things which we take for granted,
and we should continually praise our God,
who is true to His promise, who has provided
and retained the necessities for our living.

BETTY FUHRMAN

A Treasury of Faith

Faith expects from God
what is beyond all expectations.

Sisters that hold each other accountable usually
have a deep, abiding, and open relationship….
Being aware that a sister cares enough to make us
accountable creates a stronger bond.

*If it can be verified, we don't need faith….
Faith is for that which lies on the other side
of reason. Faith is what makes life bearable,
with all its tragedies and ambiguities and
sudden, startling joys.*

MADELEINE L'ENGLE

For I am bound with fleshly bands,
Joy, beauty, lie beyond my scope;
I strain my heart, I stretch my hands,
And catch at hope.

CHRISTINA ROSSETTI

Be on your guard; stand firm in the faith;
be courageous; be strong.

1 CORINTHIANS 16:13 NIV

I think miracles exist in part as gifts
and in part as clues that there is
something beyond the flat world we see.

PEGGY NOONAN

Just as a prism of glass miters light
and casts a colored braid, a garden sings sweet
incantations the human heart strains to hear.
Hiding in every flower, in every leaf,
in every twig and bough, are reflections
of the God who once walked with us in Eden.

TONIA TRIEBWASSER

*F*aith is not an effort, a striving, a ceaseless
seeking, as so many earnest souls suppose,
but rather a letting go, an abandonment,
an abiding rest in God that nothing,
not even the soul's shortcomings, can disturb.

*T*he day is done, the sun has set,
Yet light still tints the sky;
My heart stands still
In reverence,
For God is passing by.

RUTH ALLA WAGER

*W*ithin each of us there is an inner place
where the living God Himself longs to dwell,
our sacred center of belief.

Ever since I first heard of your strong faith in
the Lord Jesus and your love for God's people
everywhere, I have not stopped thanking
God for you. I pray for you constantly.

EPHESIANS 1:15–16 NLT

We must drink deeply from the very Source
the deep calm and peace of interior quietude
and refreshment of God, allowing the pure water
of divine grace to flow plentifully
and unceasingly from the Source itself.

MOTHER TERESA

I believe in the sun even if it isn't shining.
I believe in love even when I am alone.
I believe in God even when He is silent.

Now faith is the substance of things hoped for,
the evidence of things not seen.

So wait before the Lord. Wait in the stillness.
And in that stillness, assurance will come to you.
You will know that you are heard;...you will hear
quiet words spoken to you yourself, perhaps to
your grateful surprise and refreshment.

AMY CARMICHAEL

Faith means being sure of what we hope for...
now. It means knowing something is real,
this moment, all around you, even when you don't
see it. Great faith isn't the ability to believe long
and far into the misty future. It's simply taking
God at His word and taking the next step.

JONI EARECKSON TADA

Heartfelt Prayers

Pour out your heart to God your Father.
He understands you better than you do.

I said a prayer for you today
And I know God must have heard,
I felt the answer in my heart
Although He spoke no word.
I asked that He'd be near you
At the start of each new day,
To grant you health and blessings
And friends to share the way.
I asked for happiness for you
In all things great and small,
But it was His loving care
I prayed for most of all.

*W*hen we call on God,
He bends down His ear to listen,
as a father bends down
to listen to his little child.

ELIZABETH CHARLES

I call on you, O God, for you will answer me;
give ear to me and hear my prayer. Show the
wonder of your great love, you who save by your
right hand those who take refuge in you.

PSALM 17:6–7 NIV

We must take our troubles to the Lord,
but we must do more than that;
we must leave them there.

HANNAH WHITALL SMITH

Though no one knows the future
My prayer will always be
While traveling on life's road
You'll be right there with me.

ALORA M. KNIGHT

You pay God a compliment by asking great things of Him

TERESA OF AVILA

If a care is too small
to be turned into a prayer
then it is too small
to be made into a burden.

You help us by your prayers.
Then many will give thanks
on your behalf for the gracious favor
granted us in answer to the prayers of many.

2 CORINTHIANS 1:11 NIV

*L*ord...give me the gift of faith
to be renewed and shared
with others each day.
Teach me to live this moment only,
looking neither to the past with regret,
nor the future with apprehension.
Let love be my aim and my life a prayer.

ROSEANN ALEXANDER-ISHAM

*W*e need quiet time to examine
our lives openly and honestly...
spending quiet time alone
gives your mind an opportunity
to renew itself and create order.

SUSAN L. TAYLOR

God bless the friend who sees my needs
and reaches out a hand,
who lifts me up, who prays for me,
and helps me understand.

AMANDA BRADLEY

It is when things go wrong,
when good things do not happen,
when our prayers seem to have been lost,
that God is most present.

MADELEINE L'ENGLE

As soon as I pray, you answer me;
you encourage me by giving me strength.

PSALM 138:3 NLT

Family Connections

Within the property of our heart and soul
we find our sister; she is essential to our memories,
our connectedness, our being.

Call it clan, call it a network, call it a tribe,
call it a family. Whatever you call it,
whoever you are, you need one.

JANE HOWARD

It's hard to be responsible, adult, and sensible
all the time. How good it is to have a sister whose
heart is as young as your own.

PAM BROWN

As for me and my house, we will serve the LORD.

JOSHUA 24:15 NASB

We know one another's faults, virtues,
catastrophes, mortifications, triumphs, rivalries,
desires, and how long we can each hang by our
hands to a bar. We have been banded together
under pack codes and tribal laws.

ROSE MACAULAY

Family faces are magic mirrors. Looking at people who belong to us, we see the past, present, and future.

GAIL LUMET BUCKLEY

Having a sister is like having a best friend you can't get rid of. You know whatever you do, they'll still be there.

AMY LI

Please, bless my family. Let it continue before you always. Lord God, you have said so.

2 SAMUEL 7:29 NCV

Like branches on a tree we grow in different directions, yet our roots remain as one. Each of our lives will always be a special part of the other.

We were a strange little band of characters, trudging through life sharing diseases and toothpaste, coveting one another's desserts, hiding shampoo, borrowing money, locking each other out of our rooms, inflicting pain and kissing to heal it in the same instant, loving, laughing, defending, and trying to figure out the common thread that bound us all together.

ERMA BOMBECK

The effect of having other interests beyond those domestic works well. The more one does and sees and feels, the more one is able to do, and the more genuine may be one's appreciation of fundamental things like home, and love, and understanding companionship.

AMELIA EARHART

You are fellow citizens with the saints, and are of God's household.

EPHESIANS 2:19 NASB

Sisters is probably *the* most competitive
relationship within the family, but once the sisters
are grown, it becomes the strongest relationship.

MARGARET MEAD

We really need only five things
on this earth: Some food, some sun,
some work, some fun, and someone.

BEATRICE NOLAN

Children of the same family, the same blood,
with the same first associations and habits,
have some means of enjoyment in their power,
which no subsequent connections can supply.

JANE AUSTEN

Sooner or later we all discover that
the important moments in life are not
the advertised ones, not the birthdays,
the graduations, the weddings, not the great
goals achieved. The real milestones are less
prepossessing. They come to the door of memory.

SUSAN B. ANTHONY

Families give us many things—
love and meaning, purpose and an opportunity
to give, and a sense of humor.

I find that as I grow older,
I love those most whom I loved first.

THOMAS JEFFERSON

Our Priorities

A sister listens to your deepest hurts
and feels they are hers too.

Choices can change our lives profoundly.
The choice to mend a broken relationship,
to say yes to a difficult assignment,
to lay aside some important work to play with
a child, to visit some forgotten person—
these small choices may affect our lives eternally.

GLORIA GAITHER

*Getting things accomplished isn't nearly
as important as taking time for love.*

JANETTE OKE

So be careful how you live. Don't live like fools,
but like those who are wise. Make the most of
every opportunity in these evil days.
Don't act thoughtlessly, but understand
what the Lord wants you to do.

EPHESIANS 5:15–17 NLT

Teach me, Father, to value each day,
to live, to love, to laugh, to play.

KATHI MILLS

We must not, in trying to think about how we
can make a big difference, ignore the small daily
differences we can make which, over time, add up
to big differences that we often cannot foresee.

MARIAN WRIGHT EDELMAN

The least of things with a meaning is worth more
in life than the greatest of things without it.

Be still, and in the quiet moments,
listen to the voice of your heavenly Father.
His words can renew your spirit...no one knows
you and your needs like He does.

JANET WEAVER SMITH

If I do one good thing today—
for myself, for a sister or brother, for the world—
the day will be of value.

Make the most of every opportunity.
Be gracious in your speech.
The goal is to bring out the best in others.

COLOSSIANS 4:5 MSG

Blessed is the person who is too busy to worry
in the daytime and too sleepy to worry at night.

CAROLINE SCHROEDER

Though two children have the same parents,
the same values, the same everything, they turn
out different. Isn't that the genius of God?

A good example has twice
the value of good advice.

*Live each day the fullest you can,
not guaranteeing there'll be a tomorrow,
not dwelling endlessly on yesterday.*

JANE SEYMOUR

*You will seek Me and find Me,
when you search for Me with all your heart.*

JEREMIAH 29:13 NKJV

*See each morning a world made anew,
as if it were the morning of the very first day;...
treasure and use it, as if it were
the final hour of the very last day.*

FAY HARTZELL ARNOLD

*In some families, *please* is described as the
magic word. In our house, however, it was *sorry*.*

MARGARET LAURENCE

73

If nothing seems to go my way today,
this is my happiness: God is my Father
and I am His child.

BASILEA SCHLINK

Time is a very precious gift of God; so precious
that it's only given to us moment by moment.

AMELIA BARR

Older sisters...listen to your secrets and anxieties.
And never tell—without your say-so.
An older sister is a friend and a defender—
a listener, conspirator,
a counselor and a sharer of delights....

A younger sister...is a valuable addition....
Someone who trusts you to defend her.
Someone who thinks you know
the answers to almost everything.

PAM BROWN

Bonded in Friendship

Chance made us sisters, choice made us friends. Our hearts have bonded in a friendship that is full, rich, and soul-satisfying.

Friendship is the fruit gathered from the trees planted in the rich soil of love, and nurtured with tender care and understanding.

ALMA L. WEIXELBAUM

We should all have one person who knows how to bless us despite the evidence.

PHYLLIS THEROUX

If we would build on a sure foundation in friendship, we must love friends for their sake rather than for our own.

CHARLOTTE BRONTË

Friends come and friends go,
but a true friend sticks by you like family.
PROVERBS 18:24 MSG

Some friendships last a long, long time
While others quickly end,
but to have a loving sister
is to have a lifetime friend.

Don't walk in front of me—I may not follow.
Don't walk behind me—I may not lead.
Walk beside me—And just be my friend.

I am only as strong as the coffee I drink,
the hairspray I use, and the friends I have.

Two people are better off than one, for they
can help each other succeed. If one person falls,
the other can reach out and help.

ECCLESIASTES 4:9–10 NLT

A sister never asks you for a reason,
She never asks you why, or when?
A sister pays no heed to time or season,
She's a friend.
A sister never asks for only smiles and laughter,
She's there in gladness or in tears.
A sister's there, tomorrow and hereafter,
Through the years.

*Knowing what to say is not always
necessary; just the presence of a caring friend
can make a world of difference.*

SHERI CURRY

*Insomuch as any one pushes you nearer to God,
he or she is your friend.*

FRENCH PROVERB

78

Perhaps you'd be a bit surprised how often,
if you knew,
A joke, a song, a memory will make
me think of you.
It's like another moment that we've
really spent together,
Reminding me a sister is a friend
who's there forever.

The pleasantness of a friend springs
from their heartfelt advice.

PROVERBS 27:9 NIV

Our roots say we're sisters,
our hearts say we're friends.

A friend understands what you are trying to say...
even when your thoughts aren't fitting into words.

ANN D. PARRISH

A friend hears the song in my heart and sings
it to me when my memory fails.

*L*ine by line, moment by moment,
special times are etched into our memories
in the permanent ink of everlasting relationships.

GLORIA GAITHER

*W*hen hands reach out in friendship,
hearts are touched with joy.

*H*aving someone who understands is a great
blessing for ourselves. Being someone who
understands is a great blessing to others.

JANETTE OKE

*Y*our life is the answer to someone's prayers.

Provisions in Full Measure

Sisters are beyond price,
and there is no measuring of their goodness.

My sister's hands are fair and white;
my sister's hands are dark.
My sister's hands are touched with age,
or by the years unmarked.
And often when I pray for strength to live
as He commands
The Father sends me sustenance
in my sister's hands.

*If you have a special need today,
focus your full attention on the goodness
and greatness of your Father rather than on
the size of your need. Your need is so small
compared to His ability to meet it.*

Sisters are angels who lend us their wings when
our wings have forgotten how to fly.

A father to the fatherless,
a defender of widows,
is God in his holy dwelling.
God sets the lonely in families,
he leads forth the prisoners with singing....
You gave abundant showers,
O God; you refreshed your weary inheritance.
Your people settled in it,
and from your bounty,
O God, you provided for the poor.

PSALM 68:5–6, 9–10 NIV

*T*here will be days which are great
and everything goes as planned.
There will be other days when
we aren't sure why we got out of bed.
Regardless of which kind of day it is,
we can be assured that
God takes care of our daily needs.

EMILIE BARNES

God's gifts make us truly wealthy.
His loving supply never shall leave us wanting.

BECKY LAIRD

*One of the best things about being an adult
is the realization that you can share with
your sister and still have plenty for yourself.*

BETSY COHEN

You can trust God right now to supply all
your needs for today. And if your needs are
more tomorrow, His supply will be greater also.

Provide me with the insight
that comes only from Your Word.

PSALM 119:169 MSG

You care for the land and water it; you enrich it abundantly. The streams of God are filled with water to provide the people with grain, for so you have ordained it.

PSALM 65:9 NIV

Throughout the Bible, when God asked a man to do something, methods, means, materials and specific directions were always provided. The man had one thing to do: obey.

ELISABETH ELLIOT

I must simply be thankful, and I am, for all the Lord has provided for me, whether big or small in the eyes of someone else.

MABEL P. ADAMSON

A sister by your side can keep you warmer than the most expensive coat.

You know full as well as I do
the value of sisters' affections to each other;
there is nothing like it in this world.

CHARLOTTE BRONTË

It is not my business to think about myself.
My business is to think about God.
It is for God to think about me.

SIMONE WEIL

God provides resting places
as well as working places.
Rest, then, and be thankful

when He brings you, wearied,
to a wayside well.

L. B. COWMAN

Celebrating Our Gifts

A true friend inspires you to believe the best in yourself, to keep pursuing your deepest dreams—most wonderful of all, she celebrates all your successes as if they were her own!

Since you are like no other being ever created since the beginning of time, you are incomparable.

BRENDA UELAND

God does not ask your ability or your inability. He asks only your availability.

MARY KAY ASH

Each one of us is God's special work of art. Through us, He teaches and inspires, delights and encourages, informs and uplifts all those who view our lives.

JONI EARECKSON TADA

Receiving a gift is like getting a rare gemstone; any way you look at it, you see beauty refracted.

PROVERBS 17:8 MSG

My sister is my future.
She lives within my dreams
She sees my undiscovered secrets,
Believes in me as I stumble
She walks in step beside me,
Her love lighting my way.

LISA LORDEN

*God's designs regarding you,
and His methods of bringing about
these designs, are infinitely wise.*

MADAME JEANNE GUYON

Both within the family and without, our sisters
hold up our mirrors, our images of who we are
and of who we can dare to become.

ELIZABETH FISHEL

Give, and it will be given to you.
A good measure, pressed down,
shaken together and running over,
will be poured into your lap.
For with the measure you use,
it will be measured to you.

LUKE 6:38 NIV

This is the real gift: you have been given
the breath of life, designed with a unique,
one-of-a-kind soul that exists forever—
the way that you choose to live it doesn't change
the fact that you've been given the gift of
being now and forever. Priceless in value,
you are handcrafted by God,
who has a personal design and plan for each of us.

Many persons have a wrong idea
of what constitutes true happiness.
It is not attained through self-gratification
but through fidelity to a worthy purpose.

HELEN KELLER

When I stand before God at the end of my
life, I would hope that I would not have
a single bit of talent left and could say, "
I used everything You gave me."

ERMA BOMBECK

From his abundance we have all received
one gracious blessing after another.

JOHN 1:16 NLT

God has designs on our future...
and He has designed us for the future.
He has given us something to do
in the future that no one else can do.

RUTH SENTER

God gave me my gifts. I will do all I can
to show Him how grateful I am to Him.

GRACE LIVINGSTON HILL

There are no limits to our opportunities.
Most of us see only a small portion of what is
possible. We create opportunities by seeing
the possibilities and having the persistence
to act upon them. We must always remember...
opportunities are always here,
but we must look for them.

Sweet Simplicity

Sisters find the sweetest sense of happiness
comes from simply being together.

We should never let ourselves get so busy that we
miss those little but important extras in life—
the beauty of a day...the smile of a friend...
the serenity of a quiet moment alone.
For it is often life's smallest pleasures and
gentlest joys that make the biggest
and most lasting difference.

From the simple seeds of understanding,
we reap the lovely harvest of true friendship.

Not every day of our lives is overflowing
with joy and celebration. But there are moments
when our hearts nearly burst within us
for the sheer joy of being alive. The first sight
of our newborn babies, the warmth of love
in another's eyes, the fresh scent of rain on
a hot summer's eve—moments like these
renew in us a heartfelt appreciation for life.

GWEN ELLIS

Let us consider how we may spur one another on toward love and good deeds, not giving up meeting together, as some are in the habit of doing, but encouraging one another.

HEBREWS 10:24–25 NIV

It's simple things, like a glowing sunset,
the sound of a running stream
or the fresh smell in a meadow
that cause us to pause and marvel
at the wonder of life, to contemplate
its meaning and significance.
Who can hold an autumn leaf
in their hand, or sift the warm white sand
on the beach, and not wonder
at the Creator of it all?

*Enjoy the little things. One day you may look
back and realize...they were the big things.*

*As different as my sister and I are,
I need only to look in the mirror and I see her
eyes, her mouth, her expression;
then I remember all that we have in common.*

LAURIE HARPER

*A simple life in the Fear-of-God is better
than a rich life with a ton of headaches.*

PROVERBS 15:16 MSG

*My sister taught me everything
I really need to know, and she was only
in sixth grade at the time.*

LINDA SUNSHINE

A fiery sunset, tiny pansies by the wayside,
the sound of raindrops tapping on the roof—
what extraordinary delight we find in the simple
wonders of life! With wide eyes and full hearts,
we may cherish what others often miss.

When you're growing up, a sister can be
a ready-made playmate...in old age,
you've got someone who doesn't get bored
by all your stories of the "good old days."

JANE DOWDESWELL

It isn't the great big pleasures that count the
most; it's making a great deal out of the little ones.

JEAN WEBSTER

There's a special kind of freedom sisters enjoy.
Freedom to share innermost thoughts,
to ask a favor, to show their true feelings.
The freedom to simply be themselves.

So in everything, do to others what
you would have them do to you,
for this sums up the Law and the Prophets.

MATTHEW 7:12 NIV

Happy people...enjoy the fundamental,
often very simple things of life....
They savor the moment, glad to be alive,
enjoying their work, their families,
the good things around them.
They are adaptable;
they can bend with the wind,
adjust to the changes in their times,
enjoy the contest of life....
Their eyes are turned outward;
they are aware, compassionate.
They have the capacity to love.

JANE CANFIELD

God Our Father

Because I have known you, my sister,
I know more of my God.

The God who created, names, and numbers the stars in the heavens also numbers the hairs of my head.... He pays attention to very big things and to very small ones. What matters to me matters to Him, and that changes my life.

ELISABETH ELLIOT

The treasure our heart searches
for is found in the ocean of God's love.
JANET WEAVER SMITH

My Sister's Hands

My sister's hands: compassion's tools
that teach my own their art
Witnesses of charity within the human heart
Bearers of the Savior's love and mercy unto man
I have felt the Master's touch in my sister's hands.

Incredible as it may seem, God wants our
companionship. He wants to have
us close to Him. He wants to be a father to us,
to shield us, to protect us, to counsel us,
and to guide us in our way through life.
BILLY GRAHAM

Stand outside this evening.
Look at the stars. Know that you are special
and loved by the One who created them.

Steep yourself in God-reality,
God-initiative, God-provisions.
You'll find all your everyday human
concerns will be met. Don't be afraid
of missing out. You're my dearest friends!
The Father wants to give you
the very kingdom itself.

LUKE 12:31–32 MSG

The Creator thinks enough of you
to have sent Someone very special
so that you might have life—abundantly,
joyfully, completely, and victoriously.

Before anything else, above all else,
beyond everything else, God loves us.
God loves us extravagantly, ridiculously,
without limit or condition.
God is in love with us...God yearns for us.

ROBERTA BONDI

*God will never let you be shaken
or moved from your place near His heart.*

JONI EARECKSON TADA

When you love someone, you give to them,
as God gives to us. The greatest gift
He ever gave was the person of His Son,
sent to us in human form so that we
might know what God the Father is really like!

DALE EVANS ROGERS

We continually recall before
God our Father the things you
have done because of your faith
and the work you have done
because of your love.

1 THESSALONIANS 1:3 NCV

God is every moment totally aware of each one
of us. Totally aware in intense concentration
and love.... No one passes through any area of life,
happy or tragic, without the attention of God.

EUGENIA PRICE

As a rose fills a room with its fragrance,
so will God's love fill our lives.

MARGARET BROWNLEY

Whoever walks toward God one step,
God runs toward him two.

JEWISH PROVERB

Thank You, Father, for loving all
the little children of the world—
no matter how old we are.

MARION BOND WEST

Those who know God as their Father
know the whole secret. They are His heirs,
and may enter now into possession
of all that is necessary for their present needs.

HANNAH WHITALL SMITH

The Truth Is...

There's a special kind of freedom sisters enjoy.
Freedom to share innermost thoughts,
to ask a favor, to show their true feelings.
The freedom to simply be themselves.

Love is here and now, real and true,
the most important thing in our lives.
For love is the creator of our favorite memories
and the foundation of our fondest dreams.
Love is a promise that is always kept,
a fortune that can never be spent, a
seed that can flourish in even the most unlikely
of places. And this radiance that never fades,
this mysterious and magical joy,
is the greatest treasure of all—
one known only by those who love.

Go after a life of love as if your life
depended on it—because it does.
Give yourselves to the gifts God gives you.
Most of all, try to proclaim his truth.

1 Corinthians 14:1 msg

The one who comes from above is above all.

JOHN 3:31 NIV

Amid ancient lore the Word of God stands
unique and pre-eminent. Wonderful in its
construction, admirable in its adaptation, it
contains truths that a child may comprehend, and
mysteries into which angels desire to look.

FRANCES ELLEN WATKINS HARPER

My sister is my past.
She writes my history
In her eyes I recognize myself,
Memories only we can share.
She remembers, she forgives
She accepts me as I am
With tender understanding.

LISA LORDEN

I am amazed by the sayings of Christ.
They seem truer than anything I have ever read.
And they certainly turn the world upside down.

KATHERINE BUTLER HATHAWAY

*We may look old and wise
to the outside world. But to each other,
we are still in junior [high] school.*

CHARLOTTE GRAY

Then Jesus said..., "If you abide in My word,
you are My disciples indeed. And you shall know
the truth, and the truth shall make you free."

JOHN 8:31–32 NKJV

Open my eyes that I may see
Glimpses of truth Thou hast for me.
Place in my hands the wonderful key
That shall unclasp and set me free:
Silently now I wait for Thee,
Ready my God, Thy will to see,
Open my eyes, illumine me,
Spirit divine!

CLARA H. SCOTT

We shared. Parents. Home. Pets.
Celebrations. Catastrophes. Secrets.
And the threads of our experience became
so interwoven that we are linked.
I can never be utterly lonely,
knowing you share the planet.
I need news of you.
I need to know you're safe. I need you.

PAM BROWN

Truth is always exciting. Speak it, then.
Life is dull without it.

PEARL S. BUCK

It is an extraordinary and beautiful
thing that God, in creation...works with the
beauty of matter; the reality of things;
the discoveries of the senses, all five of them;
so that we, in turn, may hear the grass growing;
see a face springing to life in love and laughter....
The offerings of creation...our glimpses of truth.

MADELIENE L'ENGLE

Far away, there in the sunshine,
are my highest aspirations. I may not reach
them but I can look up and see their beauty,
believe in them, and try to follow where they lead.

LOUISA MAY ALCOTT

A Grateful Spirit

Happiness is a healthy mental attitude,
a grateful spirit, a clear heart full of love.

Thank You, Lord, for this chance
to stretch some more in Your direction—
to trust You when I cannot understand.

QUIN SHERRER

To receive a gift, molded from love and sacrifice,
selected with care and tied up with all the
excitement the giver has to offer,
is indeed rare. They don't come along often,
but when they do, cherish them.

ERMA BOMBECK

Seeing our Father in everything
makes life one long thanksgiving
and gives a rest of heart, and, more than
that, a gayety of spirit, that is unspeakable.
HANNAH WHITALL SMITH

Were there no God we would be in this glorious
world with grateful hearts and no one to thank.

CHRISTINA ROSSETTI

Let the peace of Christ rule in your hearts,
since as members of one body you were
called to peace. And be thankful. Let the word
of Christ dwell in you richly as you teach and
admonish one another with all wisdom through
psalms, hymns and songs from the Spirit,
singing to God with gratitude in your hearts.

COLOSSIANS 3:15–16 NIV

That I am here is a wonderful mystery
to which I will respond with joy.

*G*ratitude for the seemingly insignificant—
a seed—this plants the giant miracle.

ANN VOSKAMP

*F*eeling grateful or appreciative
of someone or something in your life
actually attracts more of the things that you
appreciate and value into your life.
And, the more of your life that you like
and appreciate, the healthier you'll be.

CHRISTIANE NORTHRUP

I thank you for answering my prayer
and giving me victory!

PSALM 118:21 NLT

A wonderful sister, a special friend,
that's what you've been to me...
so much a part of lovely times
I keep in memory.

*Y*ou are a creation of God unequaled anywhere
in the universe.... Thank Him for yourself and
then for all the rest of His glorious handiwork.

NORMAN VINCENT PEALE

*A*lmighty, most holy, most high God,
thank You for paying attention to small things.
Thank You for valuing the insignificant.
Thank You for being interested in the lilies
of the field and the birds of the air.
Thank You far caring about me. Amen.

RICHARD J. FOSTER

Most of the people I know who have
what I want—which is to say, purpose,
heart, balance, gratitude, joy—are people
with a deep sense of spirituality….
They are part of something beautiful.

ANNE LAMOTT

Thank you for the treasure of your friendship...
for showing me God's special heart of love.

Gratitude unlocks the fullness of life.
It turns what we have into enough, and more….
It can turn a meal into a feast, a house into
a home, a stranger into a friend. Gratitude
makes sense of our past, brings peace for today,
and creates a vision for tomorrow.

MELODY BEATTIE

Walking Through Life

Walking through life with a sister gives you a special kind of counterpart—someone who reflects you so intrinsically but is still her own self.

The blossom cannot tell what becomes
of its fragrance as it drifts away, just as no person
can tell what becomes of her influence
as she continues through life.

An older sister helps one remain half child,
half woman.

*Kindness is the only service that will
stand the storm of life and not wash out.
It will wear well and be remembered
long after the prism of politeness or the
complexion of courtesy has faded away.*

Sisters are our peers, the voice of our times.

Elizabeth Fishel

118

Trust in the LORD with all your heart, and lean not on your own understanding; in all your ways acknowledge Him, and He shall direct your paths.

PROVERBS 3:5–6 NKJV

What we feel, think, and do this moment influences both our present and the future in ways we may never know. Begin. Start right where you are. Consider your possibilities and find inspiration... to add more meaning and zest to your life.

ALEXANDRA STODDARD

Some people make the world special just by being in it.

The instructions of the LORD are perfect, reviving the soul. The decrees of the LORD are trustworthy, making wise the simple.

PSALM 19:7 NLT

A sister is dear to you always,
for she is someone who is always a part
of all the favorite memories
that you keep very close to your heart.

How blessed the man you train, GOD, the woman
you instruct in your Word, providing a circle of
quiet within the clamor of evil.... God will never
walk away from his people, never desert his
precious people. Rest assured that justice is on its
way and every good heart put right.

PSALM 94:12–15 MSG

*The real secret of happiness is not what you
give or what you receive, it's what you share.*

120

Sisters—they share the agony and
the exhilaration. As youngsters they may share
popsicles, chewing gum, hair dryers,
and bedrooms. When they grow up,
they share confidences, careers and children,
and some even chat for hours every day.

ROXANNE BROWN

The fullness of our heart is expressed
in our eyes, in our touch, in what we write,
in what we say, in the way we walk,
the way we receive, the way we need.

MOTHER TERESA

Little acts of kindness which we render
to each other in everyday life, are like
flowers by the way-side to the traveler:
they serve to gladden the heart and
relieve the tedium of life's journey.

EUNICE BATHRICK

To be alive, to be able to see, to walk,
to have a home, music, paintings, friends—
it's all a miracle. I have adopted the technique
of living life from miracle to miracle.

ARTUR RUBINSTEIN

I will let God's peace infuse every part of today.
As the chaos swirls and life's demands pull at me
on all sides, I will breathe in God's peace that
surpasses all understanding.

My sister's love is very special,
one I'll treasure through the years.
We've played and laughed together
and ofttimes shed many tears.
but through life's maze of problems,
God placed a bond of love within
To unite our hearts in wisdom
changing sisters into friends.

JUDY MEGGERS

The Way of Wisdom

The wise don't expect to find life worth living;
they make it that way.

My sister is my soul.
She inspires my wearied spirit
To fly on wings of angels
But while I hold her hand
My feet never leave the ground.
She stills my deepest fears
With the wisdom of her song.

LISA LORDEN

With Him are wisdom and strength,
He has counsel and understanding.

JOB 12:13 NKJV

I am convinced beyond a shadow
of any doubt that the most valuable pursuit
we can embark upon is to know God.

KAY ARTHUR

*O*pen wide the windows of our spirits
and fill us full of light; open wide the door
of our hearts that we may receive and entertain
Thee with all the powers of our adoration.

CHRISTINA ROSSETTI

A wise gardener plants her seeds,
then has the good sense not to dig them up
every few days to see if a crop is on the way.
Likewise, we must be patient as God brings
the answers...in His own good time.

QUIN SHERRER

*T*he wisdom from above is first of all pure.
It is also peace loving, gentle at all times,
and willing to yield to others.
It is full of mercy and good deeds.

JAMES 3:17 NLT

My sister often knows the worst about me,
but she always believes in the best.

At the end of your life, you will never regret
not having passed one more test, not winning
one more verdict, or not closing one more deal.
You will regret time not spent with a husband,
a sister, a child, or a parent.

BARBARA BUSH

Blessed are those who find wisdom,
those who gain understanding,
for she is far more profitable than silver
and yields better returns than gold.

PROVERBS 3:13–14 NIV

Guide her with wisdom and gentle persuasion,
For she is God's pleasure His flower of creation.

Sisters touch your heart in ways no other could.
Sisters share...their hopes, their fears,
their love, everything they have.
Real friendship springs from their special bonds.

CARRIE BAGWELL

God wants us to be present where we are.
He invites us to see and to hear
what is around us and, through it all,
to discern the footprints of the Holy.

RICHARD J. FOSTER

Wisdom from God shows itself
most clearly in a loving heart.

LLOYD JOHN OGILVIE

Wisdom is knowing the truth,
and telling it.

Many women...have buoyed me up in times of
weariness and stress. Each friend was important....
Their words have seasoned my life.
Influence, just like salt shaken out, is hard to see,
but its flavor is hard to miss.

PAM FARREL

A sister is a person who has a sneaky knack of
saying good things about you behind your back.

What a wildly wonderful world, God! You made
it all, with Wisdom at your side, made earth
overflow with your wonderful creations.

PSALM 104:24 MSG

In Gentle Hands

In God's wisdom, He frequently chooses
to meet our needs by showing His love toward
us through the hands and hearts of others.

Jack Hayford

My sister is my strength
She hears the whispered prayers
That I cannot speak
She helps me find my smile,
Freely giving hers away
She catches my tears
In her gentle hands.

LISA LORDEN

Oh, if we did but love others! How easily
the least thing, the shutting of a door gently,
the walking softly, speaking low, not making
a noise, or the choice of a seat, so as to
leave the most convenient to others, might
become occasions of its exercise.

MÈRE ANGÉLIQUE ARNAULD

Notice words of compassion.
Seek out deeds of kindness.
These are like the doves from heaven,
pointing out to you who are the ones blessed
with inner grace and beauty.

CHRISTOPHER DE VINCK

May your footsteps set you upon
a lifetime of love.
May you wake each day with His blessings
and sleep each night in His keeping,
and may you always walk
in His tender care.

You, O Lord, are a compassionate
and gracious God,
slow to anger, abounding in love and faithfulness.

PSALM 86:15 NIV

Thank You, God, for little things
That often come our way,
The things we take for granted
But don't mention when we pray.
The unexpected courtesy,
The thoughtful kindly deed,
A hand reached out to help us
In the time of sudden need.
Oh, make us more aware, dear God,
Of little daily graces
That come to us with sweet surprise
From never-dreamed-of places.

People, even more than things,
have to be retored, renewed, revived, reclaimed,
and redeemed; never throw out anybody.

AUDREY HEPBURN

Oh the comfort—the inexpressible
comfort of feeling safe with a person—
having neither to weigh thoughts
nor measure words, but pouring them
all right out, just as they are,
chaff and grain together;
certain that a faithful hand
will take and sift them,
keep what is worth keeping, a
nd then with the breath of kindness
blow the rest away.

DINAH MARIA MULOCK CRAIK

*Each of us, made in His image
and likeness, is yet another promise
He has made to the universe that
He will continue to love it and care for it.*
BRENNAN MANNING

There isn't a man or woman anywhere,
I am convinced, who does not long for tenderness.

ELISABETH ELLIOT

Every single act of love bears the imprint of God.

We must know that we have been created for
greater things, not just to be a number in the
world, not just to go for diplomas and degrees,
this work and that work. We have been created
in order to love and to be loved.

MOTHER TERESA

Your right hand upholds me;
And Your gentleness makes me great.

PSALM 18: 35 NASB

All That's Real and Lasting

Our sweetest experiences of affection
are meant to point us to that realm which
is the real and endless home of the heart.

HENRY WARD BEECHER

Sisterhood is many things. It's a warm smile
on a cold and rainy day, a friendly hug,
a cheerful hello.... It's all that a good
and lasting friendship is, only better.
It's treasured. It's sacred. It's knowing that
there will always be someone there for you.
It's dreams shared, and goals achieved.
It's counting on others and being counted on.
It is real.

Give thanks to the LORD, for He is good!
His faithful love endures forever.

1 CHRONICLES 16:34 NLT

Allow your dreams a place in your prayers
and plans. God-given dreams can help you
move into the future He is preparing for you.

BARBARA JOHNSON

Every good action and every
perfect gift is from God.
These good gifts come down from
the Creator of the sun, moon, and stars,
who does not change like their shifting shadows.
God decided to give us life through
the word of truth so we might be the most
important of all the things He made.

JAMES 1:17–18 NCV

In the end, I think this is what
women truly desire:
to know God and to stand tall in their faith,
strong at the core, tender in heart.

RUTH SENTER

An Invitation

If you have ever:

questioned if this is all there is to life...

wondered what happens when you die...

felt a longing for purpose or significance...

wrestled with resurfacing anger...

struggled to forgive someone...

known there is a "higher power" but

couldn't define it...

sensed you have a role to play in the world...

experienced success and still felt empty afterward...

then consider Jesus.

A great teacher from two millennia ago, Jesus of Nazareth, freely chose to show our Maker's everlasting love for us by offering to take all of our flaws, darkness, and mistakes into His very body (1 Peter 2:24). The result was His death on a cross. But the story doesn't end there. God raised Him to newness of life, and invites us to believe this truth in our hearts and follow Jesus into eternal life.

If you confess with your mouth that Jesus is Lord and believe in your heart that God raised him from the dead, you will be saved. —Romans 10:9